Castl
Kni
and Dragons

Katy Pike

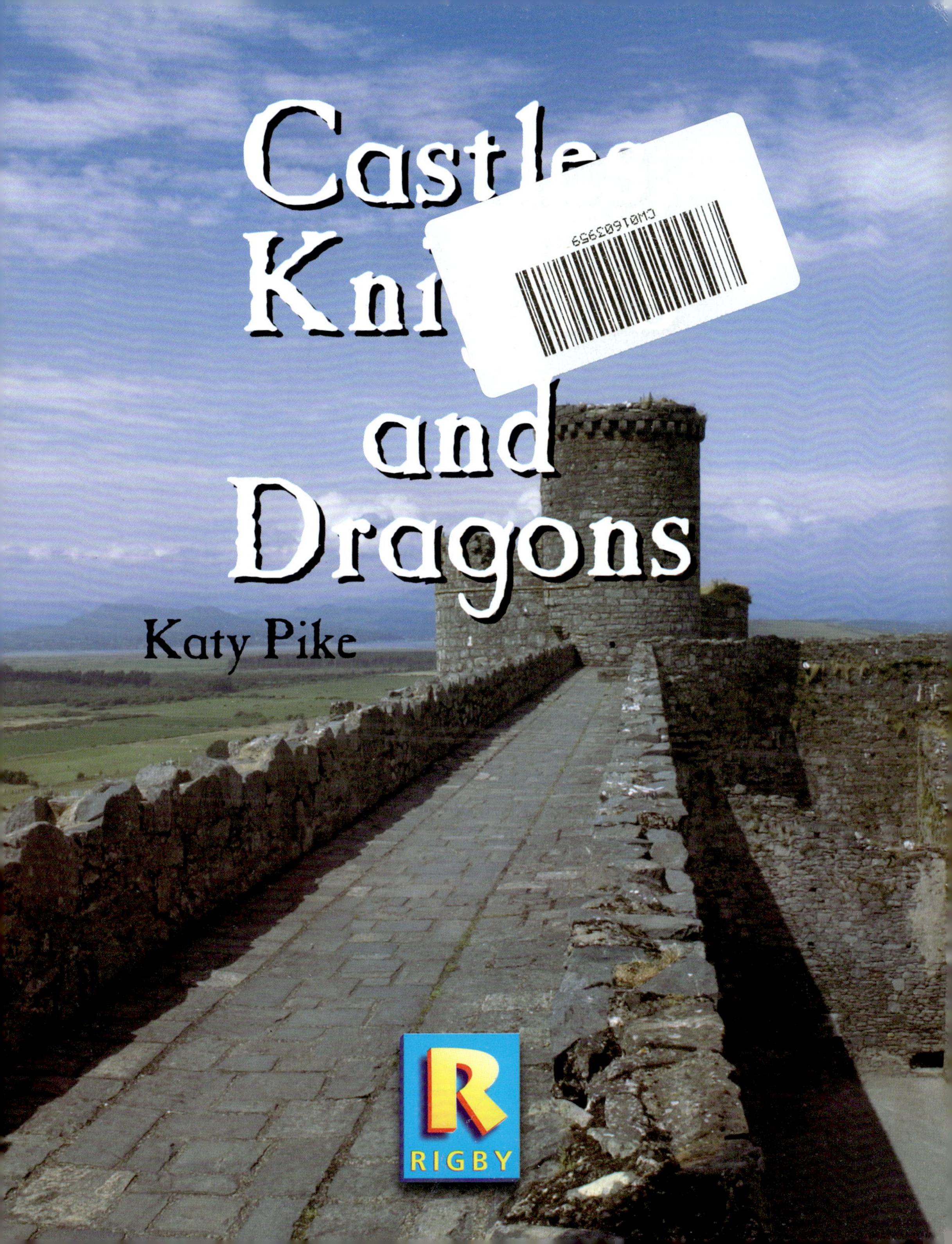

RIGBY

Contents

Castles 4

Knights 12

Dragons 20

Index 24

Castles

This castle is very old.
It is made of stone.

It was built almost a thousand years ago.

This castle is not as old as the first one.

It was built over a hundred years ago.
It is made of bricks.

This castle is in a playground.
It is made of wood.

It was built a year ago.

These castles are very small.
They are made of metal.

They are from a chess game.

This little castle is made of clay.
It is inside a fish tank.

This is not an old castle.
It is made of plastic and filled with air.

Children jump and bounce on it for fun.

These castles are built on a beach.
They are made of sand and water.

Sandcastles don't last long.
The sea comes in and knocks
them down.

Knights

Knights lived long ago.
They were soldiers and had
to fight in battles.

Knights rode horses.
The horses had to be very strong and fast.

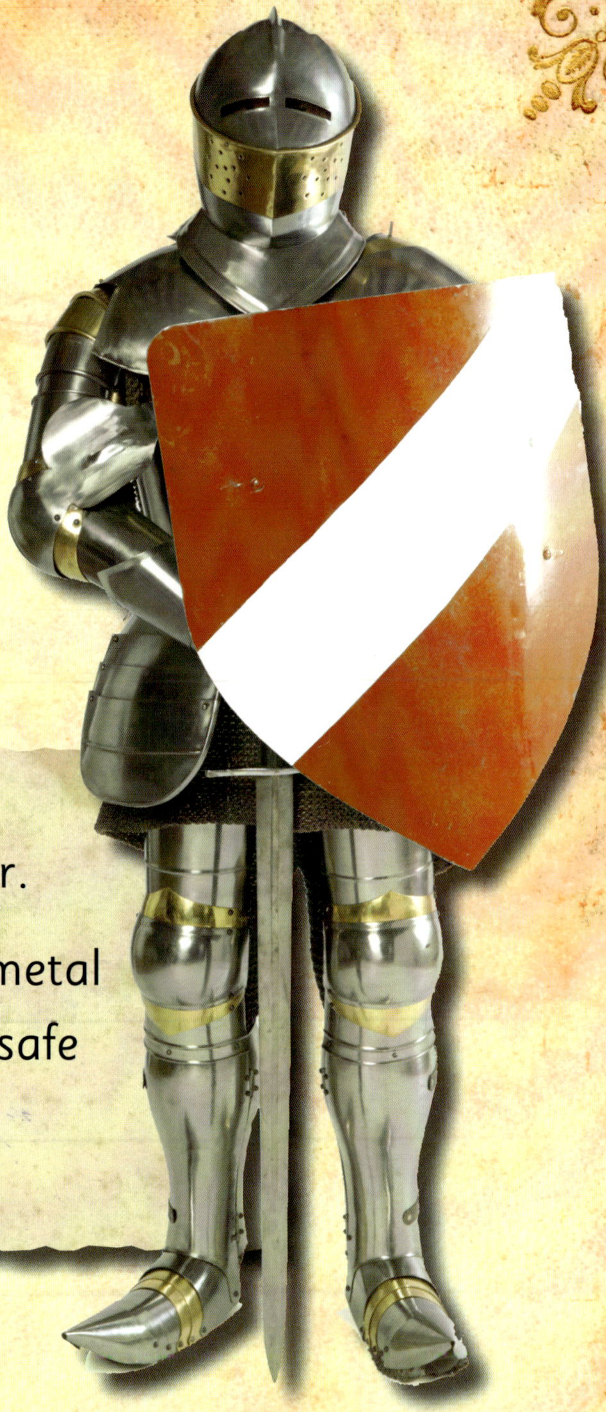

Knights wore armour.

Armour is made of metal to keep the knights safe in battle.

They also carried a shield.
The armour and the shield
protected the knight.

Jousting was a contest for knights on horses.

Two knights rode towards each
other on horses.

Each knight wore armour and carried a long lance.

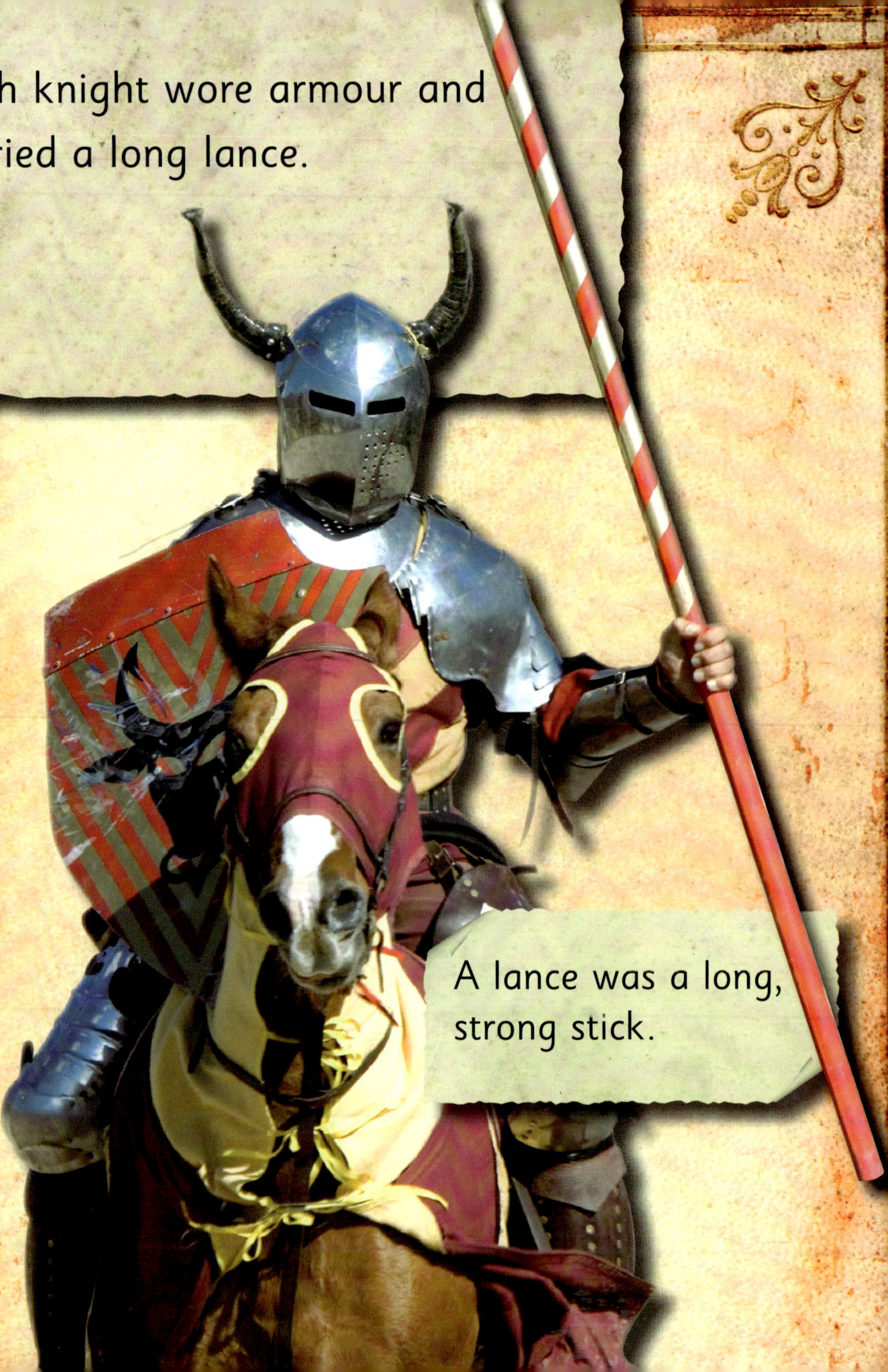

A lance was a long, strong stick.

Each knight tried to knock the other knight off his horse, with his lance.

Dragons

Dragons live in stories.

They are not real, but many people like to read about them.

In some stories, knights fight dragons.

It is hard for a knight to kill a dragon.
A dragon's skin can be as hard as metal!

This dragon is on a temple in China.

People also like to make statues of dragons.

This is a statue of a winged dragon.

Both dragons have long tails, sharp teeth and claws.

Index

armour 14-15, 18
chess.............................. 7
clay 8
horse 13, 16-19
jousting........................ 16-19
metal 7, 14, 21
plastic 9
sandcastle..................... 10-11
shield 15
statues 22-23
stories 20
wood 6